Snow Magic!

Rob Waring, *Series Editor*

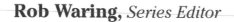

HEINLE
CENGAGE Learning™

Australia • Brazil • Japan • Korea • Mexico • Singapore • Spain • United Kingdom • United States

Words to Know

This story is set the United States (U.S.), in the state of Minnesota. It takes place in a city called Taylors Falls, which is near Minneapolis [mɪniæpəlɪs].

Minnesota
Taylors Falls
Minneapolis
CANADA
Minnesota
UNITED STATES
MEXICO
N W E S

A **Weather Words.** Here are some weather words you will find in the story. Write the letter of the correct phrase to complete the definitions.

1. Weather is _____.

2. Snow is _____.

3. Winter is _____.

4. Freeze means _____.

5. Temperature is _____.

6. Wind is _____.

a. the season when the weather is coldest

b. white, frozen water that falls from the sky

c. the level of heat or cold

d. the fast, natural movement of air

e. the conditions of the outside environment

f. to become hard at or below 0 degrees Celsius/32 degrees Fahrenheit

B **Skiing.** Read the definitions and look at the picture. Write the number of the correct <u>underlined</u> word next to each item.

1. A <u>ski run</u> is a snow-covered area that people ski on.
2. A <u>mountain</u> is a high area of land.
3. A <u>snow-making machine</u> makes artificial (not real) snow.
4. A <u>skier</u> is a person who moves on snow with long, pieces of wood or plastic, called 'skis'.

A Ski Area

The city of Minneapolis is one of the coldest places in the United States. Winter there usually lasts a very long time. However, even in winter the area sometimes has warmer weather, and that means less snow.

Most people really like this warm weather, but Dan **Raedeke**[1] doesn't like it. He doesn't like it at all! Snow is very important for Raedeke's business. If it's too warm for the snow to stay on the ground, he has a big problem!

---

[1]**Raedeke:** [rədɛki]

CD 3, Track 07

Predict

Answer the questions. Then read page 7 to check your answers.

1. What is Dan Raedeke's business?

2. What does Raedeke do to get the snow he needs?

Why does Raedeke need snow? He owns the Wild Mountain Ski Area in Taylors Falls, Minnesota. He usually tries to have the ski area completely open by **Thanksgiving**,[2] which is in November. But sometimes, warm weather and a shortage of natural snow cause problems with the ski runs. When this happens, Raedeke can't open until late December!

So, when nature doesn't make snow, Raedeke does. No, it's not **magic**.[3] Raedeke owns the largest snow-making system in the area. He says, "Without snowmaking, we could probably never open...especially in a year like this. The **fields**[4] are still brown!"

---

[2]**Thanksgiving:** a U.S. national holiday for giving thanks
[3]**magic:** special power that makes impossible things happen
[4]**field:** area of land used for growing food or keeping animals

Snow has always been a very important part of Raedeke's life. His family bought the Wild Mountain Ski Area 28 years ago. Since that time, he's spent nearly every day on the mountain. That experience has helped Raedeke a lot. In addition, Raedeke has also studied **mechanical engineering**.[5] The combination of these two things makes Raedeke kind of a 'specialist' in making snow. He really understands snowmaking and the machines that do it. "Best machine-made snow ever!" he says of his machines. "Look how great that snow is!"

---

[5]**mechanical engineering:** the study of making machines and systems

Snowmaking is kind of a science, but it's also an art, too. It's careful and detailed work. The person making the snow has to carefully measure the water, check the air temperature, and watch the wind. Raedeke explains, "if there's wind, it'll actually **blow**[6] [the water] around and allow it to freeze before it hits the ground. That's why the **snow guns**[7] are always high in the air."

---

[6] **blow:** move with air currents
[7] **snow gun:** a special machine that pushes water into the air to make snow

wind

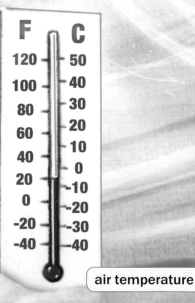

air temperature

snow

water

snow gun

Skim the previous pages and answer the questions.

1. Why does Raedeke know so much about snowmaking?

2. How does he feel about making snow with machines?

There are good things about both real and man-made snow. However, they are different. Real snow is drier, softer, and of better quality for skiing. But man-made snow lasts for a longer time when there are a lot of people skiing on it.

Raedeke depends on snow for his business. Because of this, he has some of the best snow-making technology available. His newest machines are tall, thin **poles**[8] called 'water sticks'. Raedeke selected them because they produce a lot of snow very quickly. "They make a very soft snow–almost as good as snow from the sky. In one night we can cover this entire **trail**,"[9] he reports. "They're great!" That may be why Raedeke has water sticks on half of the Wild Mountain runs.

---

[8]**pole:** a long wooden or metal rod
[9]**trail:** another word for a ski run; a path

Raedeke then talks about the building that houses the **pumps**[10] for making snow. "This is the **nerve center**[11] of the snow-making system," he says. He explains that it takes good timing to determine which ski runs need snow and which ones don't. He adds that only six pumps control the water that goes through all the **pipes**.[12]

When the water is turned off, Dave Lindgren, the mountain manager, quickly gets the water out of the system. If he doesn't, the pipes might freeze. If a pipe freezes, it's completely useless for the rest of the winter. As he does this, Lindgren also learns a good lesson. Just like all the skiers, he has to be very careful. It's easy to fall down on any kind of snow!

---

[10] **pump:** a machine that forces water to move from one place to another

[11] **nerve center:** a place from which an organization or activity is controlled or managed

[12] **pipe:** a tube through which water or other liquids pass from one place to another

pumps

pipe

People must be careful on any kind of snow!

Lindgren goes on to describe the water supply system for Wild Mountain's snow-making operation. Snowmaking needs a lot of water all of the time. So where does all of this water come from?

"This is where we get all our water," says Lindgren. He's talking about the water **reservoir**[13] on top of Wild Mountain. It's a big system. The snow-making process at the ski area needs **3,000 gallons**[14] of water every minute! The reservoir must provide all of this water day after day during warm periods in the winter months.

---

[13] **reservoir:** an man-made lake where water is stored
[14] **3,000 gallons (U.S.):** 11,356 liters

Raedeke is very careful about the snow-making process. He often spends all day and most of the night checking the system. He says, "We check the snow, and we want it like a good snowball." He then picks up a handful of snow. "You can see it's just a little bit wet, and so we'll go to the [snow] gun and turn down the water," he explains. The process requires a lot of care. If there's too much water, the snow gets soft; if there's too little water, the snow doesn't stay on the ground long enough.

To prepare for the next day, Raedeke operates the snow-making machines all night. The ski runs will be covered with new snow in the morning. Wild Mountain will be ready for the day's skiers—with or without nature's help. With good weather, and a little 'snow magic', Raedeke can keep his skiers happy all winter long!

After You Read

1. In Minneapolis, winter is _____ cold and long.
   A. generally
   B. always
   C. sometimes
   D. never

2. In paragraph 1 on page 7, the word 'completely' can be replaced by:
   A. partly
   B. possibly
   C. totally
   D. nearly

3. Dan Raedeke can't open the ski area when:
   A. The fields are still brown.
   B. The weather is warm.
   C. There is little real snow.
   D. all of the above

4. What is Raedeke's job?
   A. skier
   B. business owner
   C. mechanical engineer
   D. mountain manager

5. In the first sentence on page 10, 'it' refers to:
   A. air temperature
   B. science
   C. wind direction
   D. snowmaking

6. The writer says that snowmaking is an art because:
   A. Water, wind, and air are parts of science.
   B. The snow is artificial.
   C. People must work carefully to make great snow.
   D. The snow guns are high in the air.

7. In paragraph 2 on page 13, the word 'selected' can be replaced by:
   A. decided
   B. chose
   C. liked
   D. needed

8. Raedeke's snow-making machines are good for the following reasons EXCEPT:
   A. They are tall.
   B. They are fast.
   C. They are new.
   D. They are wide.

9. What is the purpose of the last line on page 14?
   A. to explain a surprising event
   B. to show that skiing is dangerous
   C. to worry the reader
   D. to talk about Raedeke's fall

10. When artificial snow doesn't stay on the ground long enough, what is the reason?
    A. It's too wet.
    B. There's too much water.
    C. It's too soft.
    D. There's not enough water.

11. What is NOT part of the snow-making process?
    A. care
    B. water
    C. magic
    D. snow guns

My Visit to the South Pole

December 19

This is going to be a long day. Actually, I'm going to have several very long days. In order to begin my visit to the South Pole, I have a long way to go. First, I have to get from the U.S. to McMurdo Station in Antarctica. I left the house at 5:00 this morning and I won't get to Antarctica for at least three days. It's over 9,000 miles away!

December 22

Well, I'm finally here. We arrived at McMurdo Station at 9:00 last night. It's windy and freezing cold and there is so much snow on the ground. It isn't even winter in Antarctica now! I don't know what the temperature is and I don't want to know. The people with me are a very international group–North Americans, Europeans and South Americans. Tomorrow we are leaving to go to the South Pole!

The Area around the South Pole

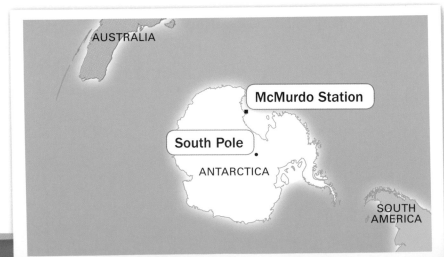

Here I am at the South Pole!

December 24

Here I am at the South Pole! The weather is unbelievably cold. It's 11:00 at night and it looks like it could be 11:00 in the morning. There is daylight here for 24 hours a day at this time of year. Can you believe I just met a group of skiers? They're from Australia and they're spending nine days skiing around Antarctica, finishing at the South Pole. I thought my trip was unusual...

December 27

I'm finally back at McMurdo Station. Thank goodness! Coming back from the South Pole wasn't as easy as getting there. The weather was bad and the wind was blowing really hard. It made getting back to the station very difficult. There were problems, but I have had a lovely time here. Right now, however, I'm so cold! My warm bed is going to be a great ending to a wonderful few days...

CD 3, Track 08

Word Count: 314
Time: _____

Vocabulary List

blow (10)
field (7)
freeze (2, 10, 14)
magic (7, 18)
mechanical engineering (8)
mountain (3, 7, 8, 13, 14, 17, 18)
nerve center (14)
pipe (14, 15)
pole (13)
pump (14, 15)
reservoir (17)
ski run (3, 7, 14, 18)
skier (3, 14, 18)
snow (2, 3, 4, 5, 7, 8, 10, 11, 12, 13, 14, 17, 18)
snow gun (10, 11)
snow-making machine (3, 18)
temperature (2, 10)
trail (13)
weather (2, 4, 7, 18)
wind (2, 10)
winter (2, 4, 14, 17, 18)